Fantasy Art

by
Mathew Jordan Assemes

About the Artist

I was born in Reading Pennsylvania in 1976 to two extraordinary people, and it's without a doubt that my hope and optimism has stemmed from their determination. I remember many times being left without electricity in the house and doing without the simplest of luxuries, but my Father's spirit and my Mother's strength held my whole world together and had eventually taken an unfortunate family to a place of stability and well-being.

I started drawing at an early age and have always been obsessed with invention and design. My room was perpetually cluttered with paper aircrafts and cardboard castles, and even in the midst of my Mother's cleaning frenzies, I managed to stash away my treasures beneath my bed and in the back of my closet. I believe that both my multi-cultured family and creativity drove an unquenchable thirst for the arts; usually leading me to hunt through my Father's book collection to study the works of Rembrandt and Parrish.

In the year 2000, I began a portrait business. I have sold hundreds of commissioned portraits from that time until now, but my love will and has always been with the world of fantasy and surrealism. I am driven to tell stories in my artwork and to piece together a place of magic. It is an endless pursuit and passion that I can't explain.

Dragonflies
Watercolor, Colored Pencil and Acrylic

See No Evil, Speak No Evil, Hear No Evil

Watercolor, Acrylic and Colored Pencil

Coy Fish

Watercolor, Colored Pencil and Acrylic

Guaramis

Watercolor, Colored Pencil and Acrylic

Sun Bathing

Acrylic

Snow Fairy

Acrylic

A Fairy Portrait

Watercolor, Acrylic and Colored Pencil

Ornament

Watercolor and Colored Pencil

Little Faces
Watercolor, Colored Pencil and Acrylic

Hidden Secrets

Acrylic

Green Apple

Acrylic

Entwined

Acrylic

Wishing Part I

Acrylic

Wishing Part II

Acrylic

Sorrow

Acrylic

Playful

Acrylic

Moods

Acrylic

At the Mulin Rouge

Acrylic

The Clocktower

Acrylic

The Air Ship
Watercolor and Colored Pencil

Morning Light

Oil on Canvas

The Phantom
The Mask Collection
Oil on Canvas

The Storm
The Mask Collection
Oil on Canvas

Guarami
The Mask Collection
Oil on Canvas

The Dance
The Mask Collection
Oil on Canvas

Masquerade
The Mask Collection
Oil on Canvas

Little Black Dress

The Mask Collection

Oil on Canvas

The Kiss

Oil on Board

About Fae Erotica

Fae Erotica is a category of my artwork that has undoubtedly raised a few eyebrows. The content is sexual in nature, and some of the pieces are explicit and raw. To me, my Fae Erotica makes perfect sense and adds balance to my art. I myself am a Father and a Husband. I have written and illustrated children's books, I have laughed at many cartoons alongside of my Sons, I do my fair share of cooking, and I go to parks with my Family to have fun and play games. But as most other people in this world, I am also a sexual being filled with passion, energy and desire. Fae Erotica has become my outlet for this passion. It has become my way of putting that energy on paper, and I find it interesting that it has reached a select audience who seems to understand it.

Adorn
Fae Erotica
Watercolor, Colored Pencil and Acrylic

Simple Pleasures
Fae Erotica
Watercolor and Colored Pencil

The Admirer
Fae Erotica
Watercolor and Colored Pencil

www.ingramcontent.com/pod-product-compliance
Lightning Source LLC
Chambersburg PA
CBHW041300180526
45172CB00003B/914